Rebecca Mansfield

It's another Quality Book from CGP

This book is for anyone doing GCSE Business Studies.

It contains lots of tricky questions designed to make you sweat — because that's the only way you'll get any better.

It's also got some daft bits in to try and make the whole experience at least vaguely entertaining for you.

What CGP is all about

Our sole aim here at CGP is to produce the highest quality books — carefully written, immaculately presented and dangerously close to being funny.

Then we work our socks off to get them out to you — at the cheapest possible prices.

Contents

Section One — Business Basics
- Why Businesses Exist 1
- Economic Systems 2
- Business Ownership Structures 3
- Franchises, Co-operatives and Public Corporations . 5
- Organisational Structure: Hierarchies 6
- Organisational Structure: Organisation Charts 7
- Measuring Business Success 8
- Stakeholders 9
- Business Basics — Important Ideas 10

Section Two — Marketing
- Marketing — What It Is 11
- Market Research 12
- Primary Research Methods 13
- The Product — Four Golden Rules 14
- Price — Demand and Supply 15
- Pricing Strategies 16
- Promotion — Advertising 17
- Promotion — Advertising Media 18
- Promotion — Other Methods 19
- Place — Where the Product is Sold 20

Section Three — Production
- Primary, Secondary and Tertiary Industry 21
- Specialisation and Interdependence 22
- Location of Production 23
- Methods of Production 24
- Organising Production 25
- Productivity and Quality Management 26

Section Four — People
- Workers 27
- Employment and the Law 28
- Motivation Theory 29
- 2 More Motivation Theories 30
- Financial Rewards 31
- Non-Financial Motivation 32
- Recruitment — Job Analysis 33
- Recruitment — the Selection Process 34
- Staff Training 35
- Trade Unions 36
- Industrial Disputes 37

Section Five — Finance
- Business Costs 38
- Break-even Analysis 39
- Internal Sources of Finance 40
- External Sources of Finance 41
- Budgeting 42
- Cash Flow 43
- The Trading, Profit and Loss Account 44
- The Balance Sheet — Net Assets 45
- The Balance Sheet — Capital Employed 46
- Analysis of Accounts — Ratios 47
- Using Ratios 48

Section Six — Growth of Firms
- Starting a New Business 49
- The Business Plan 50
- Starting a Business — Help and Support 51
- Growth of Firms — Internal Expansion 52
- Growth of Firms — Takeovers and Mergers 53
- Effects of Expansion — Economies of Scale 54
- Effects of Expansion — Communication 55
- Communication — Networks and Hierarchies 56
- Multinational Firms 57
- Competition and Monopoly 58
- The Survival of Small Firms 59
- Business Failure 60

Section Seven — External Influences
- The Business Cycle 61
- Unemployment and Inflation 62
- Government Spending and Taxation 63
- Government Economic Policy 64
- Government Policy — Consumer Protection 65
- Regional Policy 66
- Non-government Influences on Business 67
- International Trade 68
- Exchange Rates 69
- International Trade Restrictions 70
- The European Union 71
- The Single Currency and EU Laws 72

Section Eight — Business and Change
- Deindustrialisation 73
- Supply-Side Policies 74
- Flexible Working 75
- New Technology — In The Workplace 76
- New Technology — E-commerce 77
- Globalisation 78

Published by Coordination Group Publications, Ltd.

Contributors:
Peter Cunningham
Colin Harber Stuart
Pete Jarratt
Tim Major

ISBN: 978 1 84146 306 3
Groovy website: www.cgpbooks.co.uk
Jolly bits of clipart from CorelDRAW®
Printed by Elanders Hindson Ltd, Newcastle upon Tyne.
Text, design, layout and original illustrations © Coordination Group Publications Ltd. 2002
All rights reserved.

Section One — Business Basics

Why Businesses Exist

Q1 What is the most important business objective? Tick the correct answer.

- [✓] To make a profit
- [ ] To become bankrupt
- [ ] To move into the public sector

Q2 Complete the following sentences, using words from the box to fill in the spaces.

> damage   biggest   quality   objectives

Businesses will have other less important *objectives* as well as profit. Some firms will try to be the *biggest* in their market. Others will try to provide the highest *quality* products possible. Others may try to limit the environmental *damage* they cause.

Q3 How are charities different from most businesses? Write your answer in the space below.

Charities don't try to make any profit at all. Charities only need to earn enough money to cover their costs.

Q4 In the box are a number of different statements. Write them down in the table below, dividing them into statements that are true about the Public Sector or the Private Sector.

> - includes everything owned by individuals ✓
> - includes everything owned by the government ✓
> - examples include the police, the army and most schools and hospitals ✓
> - contains most of the well-known businesses ✓
> - they are provided for the benefit of everyone ✓
> - they are run for the benefit of the people who own them ✓

Public Sector	Private Sector
• includes everything owned by the goverment	• includes everything owned by individuals.
• examples include the police, the army, most schools and hospitals	• contains most of the well-known businesses
• They are provided for the benefit of everyone.	• They are run for the benefit of the people who own them.

Economic Systems

Q1 Who decides which products get made in a free-market economy?
Tick the correct answer.

- [ ] Private-sector businesses, after discussing it with the government
- [ ] The government
- [x] Private-sector businesses, if they can make a profit from making the product

Q2 Write down ONE benefit and ONE drawback of a planned economy.
Write your answers in the spaces below.

Benefit: The governments can take decisions that it believes are in the intrest of the people. For example they might want to give everyone a job, somewhere to live, free education and healthcare.

Drawback: Firms are normally not required to make a profit and so have no incentive to provide the right high quality products that people want.

Q3 Complete the following sentences, using words from the box to fill in the spaces.

> efficient ✓   welfare needs ✓   goods and services ✓
> public ✓   mixed ✓

Most countries in the world today are ....**mixed**.... economies — that is they have both a public sector and a private sector. This means that in theory they should get the best of both worlds — ....**efficient**...., competitive firms providing the ....**goods and services**.... people want and a ....**public**.... sector providing for their ....**welfare needs**.....

Section One — Business Basics

Business Ownership Structures

Q1 Which of the following is an advantage of being a sole trader? Tick the correct answer.

- [ ] A sole trader has business partners to help share the workload
- [x] A sole trader gets to decide what to do with the profits of the business
- [ ] A sole trader does not have to make a profit

Q2 Write down three disadvantages of being a sole trader. Write your answers in the spaces below.

a) you have to work long hours and you don't get many holidays off.

b) you have unlimited liability. If the business goes bust owing £10 million, you may have to sell everything you own to pay your debts.

c) If the business causes damage to something or someone, they would sue the owner of the business personally — not the business.

Q3 Tick whether the following statement is true or false. If it is false write the correct version.

> In a partnership, each partner is only legally responsible for their own business decisions.

True [ ]   False [x]

I think we'll make wonderful partners...

In a partnership, all the decisions and consaquenses are shared equally to all the business partners.

Buy your soles here — two soles for the price of one...

Setting up as a sole trader is a load easier than starting up a partnership, but it means that you have to do all the work by yourself. You pays your money, you takes your choice.

Section One — Business Basics

Business Ownership Structures

Q1 Limited companies have to produce two documents.
Write a description of the purpose of each document in the spaces below.

a) Memorandum of Association — *This tells the business world who and where the business is.*

b) Article of Association — *This sets out how the business will be run.*

Q2 Which of the following is the correct definition of limited liability? Tick the correct answer.

[✓] The maximum amount that the owners of the business can lose if the business fails. It is equal to the amount they have invested in the business.

[ ] The maximum amount that the owners of the business can lose if the business fails. It is equal to the current value of their shareholding.

Q3 Tick whether the following statement is true or false. If it is false write the correct version.

> Private Limited Companies usually become Public Limited Companies when they want to expand.

True [✓]   False [ ]

....
....

Q4 Write down TWO differences between Private Limited Companies and Public Limited Companies.

a) *Private means that shares can be sold only if all the shareholders agree. Public means that anyone can buy shares in the company.*

b) *Private limited companies usually have Ltd after the name. Public limited companies usually have Plc after the name.*

Section One — Business Basics

Franchises, Co-operatives and Public Corporations

Q1 There are two main types of franchise operation.
Write DEALER FRANCHISE or BRANDED FRANCHISE under the correct definition.

a) Firms trade under their own name but sell products made by other businesses.

   dealer franchise

b) Firms buy the right to sell products made by another business.
   The firm trades under the name of the other business.

   branded franchise

Q2 Which of the following is a benefit of franchising for the franchisee?
Tick the correct answer.

- [✓] It is less of a business risk than making and selling its own products
- [ ] It can increase its market share without increasing the size of the firm
- [ ] It may not be possible to sell products made by other firms

Q3 Complete the sentences below, using words from the box to fill in the spaces.

> capital ✓   workforce ✓   finance ✓   profits ✓
> limited liability partnerships ✓   stakeholders ✓   expand   customers ✓

Co-operatives work a bit like *limited liability partnerships*. Producer co-operatives are owned and controlled by the *workforce*. Retail co-operatives are owned and controlled by their *customers*. The main benefit is that there is no conflict between *stakeholders*. A problem is that the only main sources of *finance* are the owner's *capital* and retained *profits* — this makes it harder for the co-operative to *expand*.

Q4 Tick whether the following statement is true or false.
If it is false write the correct version.

> Public corporations do not have to make a profit
> — instead they follow objectives set by their employees.

True [ ]   False [✓]

public corporations do not have to make a profit — instead they follow objectives set by the government

Section One — Business Basics

Organisational Structure: Hierarchies

Q1 In the box are the names of four main types of person in a firm's hierarchy. Write them in order (from highest to lowest rank) in the spaces below.

> manager   shareholder   operative   director

a) shareholder

b) director

c) manager

d) ~~director~~ operatives

Q2 What is the main function of the managing director of a business? Tick the correct answer.

- [✓] To run board meetings of all the directors
- [ ] To appoint the shareholders of the business
- [✓] To run the business in between the main board meetings

Q3 Tick whether the following statement is true or false. If it's false write the correct version.

> Shareholders delegate responsibility for the general direction — the strategy — of the business to the directors.

True [✓]   False [ ]

....
....

Q4 Write down and explain three different responsibilities of managers in a business.

a) motivating - trying to keep the workers happy

b) Planning - deciding how the new factory should be built.

c) Controlling - checking the progress to make sure things will be done.

Section One — Business Basics

Organisational Structure: Organisation Charts

Q1 Which of the following is a disadvantage of organising employees by function? Tick the correct answer.

- [ ] Employees can specialise in what they are good at doing
- [x] Different departments may not work well together
- [ ] It helps the business become more customer-oriented

Q2 In the box is a description of the employees of a business. Use it to draw an organisation chart in the space below. The chart will be organised by function.

> The Marketing Director, Finance Director, Administration Director and Sales Director all report to the Managing Director.
> Each Director is responsible for the work of two managers.

Q3 Tick whether the following statement is true or false. If it is false write the correct version.

> Organising firms by process rather than function is becoming more common in the service sector – it helps the business to become more customer-oriented.

True [ ] False [ ]

....

....

Organisation — the sign of a tidy mind...

I organised my CD collection last night. It used to be in alphabetical order by artist, but I thought it would be better ordered by record label catalogue number. I think I'll go and listen to RD1029 now.

Section One — Business Basics

Measuring Business Success

Q1 Which of the following is a definition of a business strategy? Tick the correct answer.

- [ ] A measurable sales target
- [x] The way that a business co-ordinates the activities of each department in order to try and achieve its objectives
- [ ] The methods used to try and reconcile the interests of every stakeholder

Q2 Complete the sentences below, using words from the box to fill in the spaces.

> products ✓   market power ✓   market ✓
> employees ✓   sales ✓   employment ✓

Job creation is the extent to which a firm creates ...*employment*... for people.

It is usually measured by counting the number of ...*employees*... .

Market share is measured by dividing the ...*sales*... of the firm's ...*products*... into the total sales of the ...*market*... .

Basically the bigger the market share, the greater is the firm's ...*market power*... .

Q3 Write in the space below one method that a business could use to measure customer satisfaction.

...*Carrying out customer satisfaction / opinion surveys and questionaires.*...

Q4 Tick whether the following statement is true or false. If it's false write the correct version.

> Something is ethical if society believes that it is the right way to do things.

True [x]   False [ ]

Stakeholders

Q1 Write down a definition of a stakeholder in the space below.

a stakeholder is anyone who has an interest in the business.

Q2 Who are the most important stakeholders? Tick the correct answer.

- [ ] Managers
- [ ] Employees
- [x] Owners/shareholders

Q3 In the box are different stakeholders. Write them down in the table below — dividing them into internal and external stakeholders.

> owners   customers   suppliers
> employees   local community   government

Internal Stakeholders	External Stakeholders
owners	customers
employees	local community
	suppliers
	government

Q4 Complete the sentences below, using words from the box to fill in the spaces.

> sell   shareholders   directors
> ~~unproductive~~   ~~local community~~   ~~bankrupt~~

No business can ignore its customers. If it can't sell its products it will go *bankrupt*. If a business doesn't keep its workers happy it may become *unproductive*. A company may not mind being unpopular in the *local community* if it sells most of its products somewhere else. The one group no business can ignore for long is its *shareholders*. If they are unhappy they can sack the *directors* or *sell* the business to someone else.

Section One — Business Basics

Business Basics – Important Ideas

Q1 What is the difference between needs and wants? Tick the correct answer.

- [x] Our needs are limited to human survival; our wants are unlimited.
- [ ] Our needs are for luxuries; our wants are concerned with our survival.
- [ ] Needs are the things we can afford to buy; our wants are the things we can't afford.

Q2 Write down the names for the four factors of production in the spaces below.

a) Land : Natural resources

b) Labour : people

c) Capital : Equipment

d) Enterprise : Business owners

Q3 Write down a definition of opportunity cost in the space below.

Opportunity cost is the next best option we would of chosen instead.

Q4 Tick whether the following statement is true or false. If it's false write the correct version.

> Profit is the employee's reward for taking risks with their capital.

True [ ]   False [x]

Profit is the owners reward for taking risks with their capital.

You may not WANT to learn this — but you NEED to...

Not the most interesting of pages, this. Still, it's worth learning if only for the fact that without the basics there'd be no businesses — and that means no Business Studies... gulp.

Section One — Business Basics

Section Two — Marketing

Marketing — What it is

Q1 What is an accurate definition of marketing? Tick the correct answer.

☐ Marketing is how firms advertise their products.

☐ Marketing is the same as selling the product.

☑ Marketing is the art of making it as easy as possible for the potential customer to buy the product.

Q2 There are four Ps which together make up the marketing mix. Write down a description of each one in the spaces below.

P	DESCRIPTION
a) Product	The firm must come up with a product that people will want to buy. It must fulfil some of the customers wants or needs
b) Price	The customers must think the price is good value for money. This is not the same as being cheap.
c) Promotion	The product must be promoted so that potential customers are aware that it exists
d) Place	The product must be available for sale in a place that the customers will find conveniant.

Q3 Markets can be segmented into different groups of people. Write down the four different ways that people can be segmented into groups.

a) Age - for example the teenage market

b) Gender

c) Culture or religion

d) location

Q4 Complete the sentence below. Fill in the missing word.

Any firm can market its products, a successful firm will market its products and make a ......profit...... from selling them.

The four Ps — pie pie pie pie... Mmmmmmmm...

It makes sense that if you want to sell a product, it's got to be something that people actually want. I worked for a company trying to market a gas-powered nail clipper. They sold out pretty fast.

Market Research

Q1 Complete the sentences below, using words from the box to fill in the spaces.

> questionnaire ✓   expensive ✓   primary research ✓
> relevant ✓   new information ✓

Field research is also known as *primary research*. It is useful for finding out *new information* and a popular method is to use a *questionnaire*. A benefit of using field research is that the information collected is directly *relevant* to the needs of the business. A disadvantage is that the information can be very *expensive* to collect.

Q2 Which of the following are disadvantages of using desk research? Put a tick in the correct boxes.

- [ ] It is cheaper than field research
- [✓] It is not always relevant to the needs of the business
- [ ] Data can easily be found from previous research
- [✓] The data may be out of date
- [✓] The research may not be about the firm's products
- [✓] It can be very expensive because lots of people are needed to collect the data

Q3 Tick whether the following statement is true or false. If it's false, write the correct version.

> Desk research is particularly useful for looking at the whole market. It helps the business to predict the future by looking at past trends.

True [✓]   False [ ]

....
....

Q4 Write down the difference between quantitative and qualitative data in the space below.

Qualitative information is all about peoples feelings and opinions. Quantitative information is anything you can measure reduce to a number.

Section Two — Marketing

Primary Research Methods

Q1 Write down six things to think about when writing a questionnaire in the spaces below.

a) Decide what information you want to find out.
b) Decide what questions you can ask to find the information
c) Use a balance of open and closed questions.
d) Write the questions using language that is unambiguous
e) Allow the respondant to give an answer that reflects opinion
f) Avoid leading questions (ask them what they prefer.)

Q2 Explain the difference between a closed question and an open question. Write your answer in the space below.

Closed questions only allow a specific answer; open questions allow the respondant to give a more detailed answer.

Q3 Which method of sampling should be used in the following situations? Write the name of a sampling method below each description.

a) You want to make sure that 70% of the sample own a mobile phone.

Quota sampling

b) The only people you want to have in your sample are males aged 20 or under.

Target sampling

c) You want everyone in the total population to have an equal chance of being in the sample.

Random samples

Section Two — Marketing

The Product — Four Golden Rules

Q1 Explain the difference between being market-driven and product-driven. Write your answer in the space below.

Market-driven firms will use market research to find out what people want, then make it. Product-driven firms will design or invent a new product, and then try to sell it.

Q2 Draw a graph to illustrate the product life cycle on the axes below.

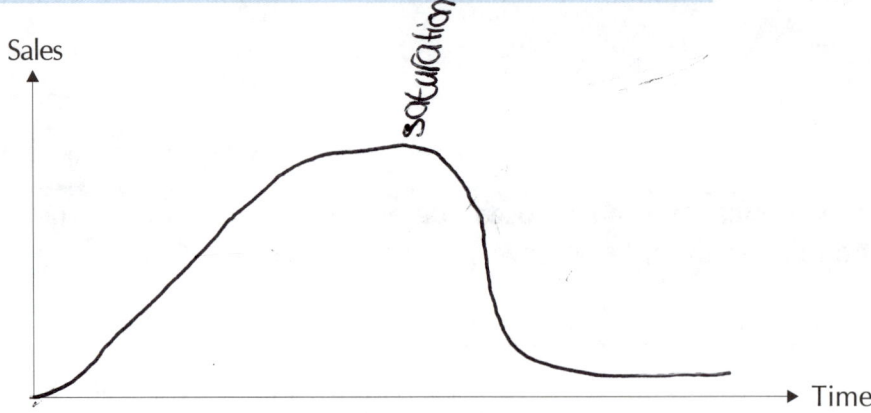

Q3 Which of the following is the correct definition of what happens at the saturation stage of the product life cycle? Tick the correct answer.

- [ ] The amount sold each week begins to increase
- [ ] The amount sold each week falls rapidly
- [x] The amount sold each week reaches a peak
- [ ] The product is taken off the market because sales are too low

Q4 How will a business benefit if it sells products that have product differentiation? Write your answer in the space below.

If all products are identical, the customer will go for the cheaper option. Products have to be unique to get more sales.

This product's life cycle is over — this is an ex-life cycle...
A lot of Business Studies is about selling products, because we're all capitalist materialists at heart. I want to buy every product that I see advertised on TV. I'm an advertiser's dream.

Section Two — Marketing

Price — Demand and Supply

Q1 Here is a list of statements about the law of demand and the law of supply. Tick the pair of statements which are **both** correct.

LAW OF DEMAND	LAW OF SUPPLY
☐ Demand increases when price increases	Supply increases when demand increases
☑ Demand decreases when price increases	Price increases when supply increases
☑ Demand increases when price decreases	Supply increases when price increases
☐ Demand increases when supply decreases	Supply increases when demand decreases

Q2 Complete the sentences below, using the words in the box to fill in the spaces.

> ~~cheaper~~   ~~afford~~   inefficient   ~~more~~
> ~~few~~   ~~profit~~   ~~low~~   high   ~~competitors~~

There are two reasons for the law of demand. At a lower price **more** people can **afford** to buy the product. The product also becomes **cheaper** compared to its **competitors**

At a low price **few** producers can make a **profit** so the supply is **low**. At a high price even .... producers can make a profit and so the supply is ....

Q3 Which of the following diagrams is the correct one? Put a tick next to the correct one.

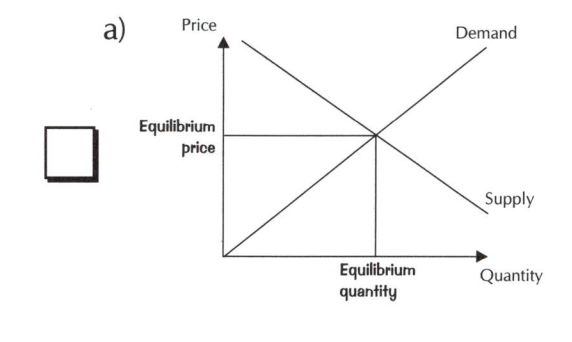

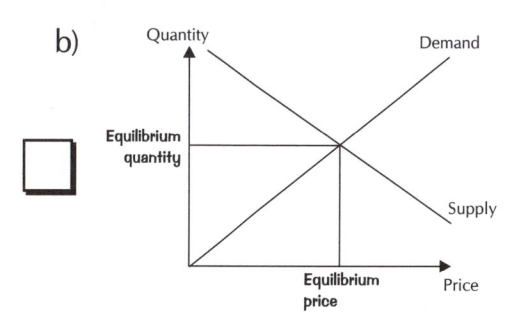

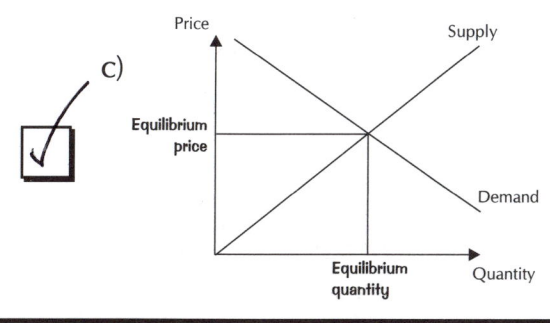

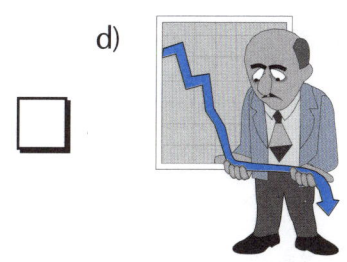

a) ☐

b) ☐

c) ☑

d) ☐

Section Two — Marketing

Pricing Strategies

Q1 Here is a list of market-led pricing strategies and a list of definitions. Match each pricing strategy to its correct definition by drawing a line.

a) Firms charge the same prices as other firms who sell similar products.

penetration pricing

b) Firms charge low prices in order to force unprofitable competitors out of the market.

skimming

c) A low price is charged to get consumers interested in the product. When sales increase the price is raised.

destroyer pricing

d) Firms charge higher prices to consumers with high incomes and lower prices to people with low incomes.

price discrimination

e) A new product is sold at a high price to make the product seem desirable. The price is then lowered to make it a mass-market product.

competition pricing

Q2 When would a firm use a cost-plus pricing method instead of a market-led pricing strategy? Write your answer in the space below.

....

....

Q3 A firm decides to add a percentage mark-up to the cost of making its products. Calculate the selling price for each of the following products. Write your answers in the final column of the table.

	Cost of making the product	% mark-up	Selling price
a)	£100	20%	....
b)	£50	50%	....
c)	£60	25%	....
d)	£85	12%	....

Q4 Explain the different ways that mark-ups and profit margin are expressed.

....

....

....

Section Two — Marketing

Promotion — Advertising

Q1 Which of the following is a correct definition of advertising? Tick the correct answer.

☐ Any message about the firm or its products that the business has paid for.

☐ Any message about the firm or its products.

Q2 Write down four reasons why a firm might advertise a product. Write your answer in the spaces below.

a) ....

b) ....

c) ....

d) ....

Q3 Where firms advertise will depend upon three factors. Explain how each of these factors affects how a firm advertises its products. Write your answers in the spaces below.

a) The target audience ....

....

....

b) The size of the market ....

....

....

c) The size of the advertising budget ....

....

....

Q4 There are two main types of advertisement. Read the two definitions below and write the correct name for each one in the space underneath it.

a) Adverts that try to convince the consumer that good things will happen if they use the product and bad things will happen if they don't.

....

b) Adverts that describe the good features of the product and leave it to the consumer to decide whether or not the product will be of use to them.

....

Section Two — Marketing

Promotion — Advertising Media

Q1 Complete the following table by writing a benefit and drawback of each of the advertising media.

	Media	Benefit	Drawback
a)	Television	....	....
b)	Radio	....	....
c)	Newspapers and magazines	....	....
d)	Posters and billboards	....	....
e)	Cinema	....	....
f)	Leaflets and junk mail	....	....
g)	Internet sites	....	....

Q2 Complete the sentences below, using words from the box to fill in the spaces.

> opportunity cost   prices   sales   products

The advantage to a firm in advertising is that it may increase ....

The disadvantage is the .... — the firm could be spending the money on making more .... , or cutting ....

Q3 Write down four different problems of advertising for society as a whole.

a) ....

b) ....

c) ....

d) ....

Section Two — Marketing

Promotion — Other Methods

Q1 Why is sales promotion also called 'below the line' promotion? Tick the correct answer.

☐ Because it cannot be seen

☐ Because it takes place below the counter in a shop

☐ Because it does not rely on published media

Q2 Match the names of the following sales promotion methods with their correct descriptions. Write the name of the correct method after each description. The names of the methods are in the box.

> discount   competition   BOGOF   product trial   point of sale advertising

Description   **Method**

a) try a new product for free   ....

b) let the customer have a second product for free when they make a purchase   ....

c) place products in a display case in a shop   ....

d) reduce the price for a short period of time   ....

e) give consumers who buy the product the chance to win a prize   ....

Q3 Write down one benefit and one drawback to a business of using personal selling to get consumers to buy its products.

a) Benefit ....

b) Drawback ....

Q4 Complete the sentences below, using words from the box to fill in the spaces.

> PR department   free publicity   product placement   PR stunts

Public relations is ...., it helps a firm to get its name and its products well known to customers. Most large businesses have a .... Its job is to make sure that any news stories about the business show it in a good light. Some news events may have been made up by the firm. These are called ....

Another way to get free publicity is to pay film companies to use your products in their films. This is called ....

Section Two — Marketing

Place — Where the Product is Sold

Q1 Write down a definition of a retailer.

Retailers specialise in selling to the consumer

Q2 Draw a diagram to show an indirect distribution channel. Include a consumer, a wholesaler, a manufacturer and retailer in your diagram.

```
            manufacturer
     ①     ②     ③     ④
     ↓     ↓     ↓     ↓
 wholesaler       |     |
     ↓     ↓     |     |
        retailer |     |
     ↓     ↓     ↓     |
         consumer      ↓
```

Q3 Tick whether the following statement is true or false. If it's false, write the correct version.

> A benefit to a manufacturer of selling their products to a wholesaler is that the wholesaler takes on the cost of storing the products.

True ✓   False ☐

Q4 Many manufacturers now sell their products to a retailer, avoiding the use of a wholesale business in the distribution channel. Write down one benefit and one drawback of this.

a) Benefit It's faster than dealing with retailers through wholesalers, and the manufacturer gets better consumer feedback.

b) Drawback It's harder for small retailers to avoid having to hold lots of stock.

I can't get any distribution channels on my TV...

It makes a big difference to a manufacturer how their product is sold. If a retailer sells the product for them, you can be sure they'll chop off a big chunk of the profit for themselves.

Section Two — Marketing

Section Three — Production

Primary, Secondary and Tertiary Industry

Q1 In the box are the names for the three sectors of industry. Write down each one in the space next to its correct definition.

> primary sector   secondary sector   tertiary sector

a) The sector that produces services: *tertiary sector*

b) The sector that produces manufactured goods: *secondary sector*

c) The sector that produces raw materials: *primary sector*

Q2 Tick whether the following statement is true or false. If it's false write the correct version.

> Raw materials are any capital resources which can be used to produce goods or services.

True ☐   False ☐

....
....

Q3 Explain ONE difference between capital goods and consumer goods. Write your answer in the space below.

....
....
....

Q4 In the box are different types of services. Write them down in the table below, dividing them into services for businesses or consumers.

> hairdressing   advertising   boat trips
> distribution of goods   restaurant meals   warehousing

	Provided mainly for businesses	Provided mainly for consumers
a)		
b)		
c)		

Section Three — Production

Specialisation and Interdependence

Q1 Use words from the box to complete the sentences.

> job　　　specialise　　　workers　　　tasks
> productivity　　　production techniques　　　efficient

The division of labour is when firms divide up their .... and get each one to do a specific .... Firms break up complex .... into a series of simple .... and get workers to .... in them. Workers may do the same task hundreds of times a day — so they get very .... at it. This improves the firm's ....

Q2 Write down THREE different problems with the division of labour.

a) ....
....

b) ....
....

c) ....
....

Q3 Draw a production chain for a jar of coffee.
Use the words in the box to help you draw the chain.

> distribution company　　　coffee factory　　　retailer
> processor　　　shipping agent　　　grower

Section Three — Production

Location of Production

Q1 Use words from the box to complete the sentences.

> customers   production   European Union   cheapest   services

All firms, whether they produce goods or .... have to decide where to locate. This often comes down to a choice between being close to their .... or producing where it is .... But there are lots of other considerations too. For example membership of the .... is persuading more firms to locate .... on mainland Europe.

Q2 Where will bulk-increasing firms wish to locate? Tick the correct answer.

☐ As close as possible to their customers

☐ As close as possible to their raw material suppliers

☐ As close as possible to the government

Q3 Complete the following sentence by writing in the missing word.

Governments often pay firms to locate in areas of high unemployment.

This is an example of .... policy.

Q4 Explain how industrial inertia is a factor influencing the location decisions of some firms.

....

....

....

....

It's all about location, location, location...

...and not just so the manufacturers get to have a nice view, either. Try and write out the 9 factors influencing the choice of location for a firm's production. Why? I thought it might be fun.

Section Three — Production

Methods of Production

Q1 Tick whether the following statement is true or false. If it's false write the correct version.

> Job production is used when a firm manufactures individual, unique products.

True ☐   False ☐

....

....

Q2 Complete the sentences below, using words from the box to complete the sentences.

> minimum unit cost   no stoppages   capital intensive
> workers   shifts   economies of scale   continuous
> make as many as possible   robots   identical

Mass production is where all products are .... and the

aim is to .... To be efficient production has to be

.... with ....

Many mass production factories operate 24 hours a day with

.... rotating in ....

The aim is to gain from .... and so produce at

.... Mass production is highly

.... — it costs a lot to buy the machinery but it's cheap

to run it afterwards. Modern mass production techniques use

.... not people to do most of the work.

Q3 Explain how batch production combines job production and mass production.

....

....

....

....

Section Three — Production

Organising Production

Q1 Write a sentence to explain how process layout production is organised.

....
....
....

Q2 Explain how assembly line production is different to process layout production.

....
....
....

Q3 Tick the sentence which explains why team production is considered to be better than a system where each worker specialises in a different task.

☐ It gives workers more variety and responsibility, so productivity should improve.

☐ It gives workers fewer tasks to do, so they become less bored.

☐ It gives workers less variety and responsibility, so productivity should improve.

Q4 In the box are the names for the two main types of team production. Write the name of each type in the space below its correct definition.

> group production   cell production

a) A team of workers are responsible for making the whole product.

....

b) A team of workers are responsible for a number of tasks at a single stage of the production process.

....

This page was made on an assembly line...

Colin wrote the words, Tim drew the pictures, Dominic crossed it all out and started again, then Paul stapled the pages together. Then right at the end I coloured in the boxes with my felt tip pen.

Section Three — Production

Productivity and Quality Management

Q1 Tick whether the following statement is true or false. If it's false write the correct version.

> Lean production is a Japanese approach to making products that aims to use as few resources as possible. Waste and stocks of raw materials are kept to a minimum.

True ☐   False ☐

....

....

Q2 Draw a stock control graph to show a product with a maximum stock level of 600, a re-order level of 400 and a minimum stock level of 200.

Stock level

Time

Q3 Use words from the box to complete the sentences.

> suppliers   bare minimum   Japanese   run out of stock
> co-ordination   reduces the cost   before

Just-in-time (JIT) is a .... method that aims to keep stock levels to the

.... The aim is that stock arrives in the factory immediately

.... it is used. The main benefit is that it .... of having

to keep stocks. The main problem is that it requires a lot of .... between

the firm and its ...., otherwise the firm could ....

Q4 There are two main methods of quality management. Write a description of each one in the spaces below.

a) Kaizen/continuous improvement: ....

....

b) Statistical process control: ....

....

Section Three — Production

Section Four — People

Workers

Q1 Write down five reasons why someone might choose to work for less money for more job satisfaction.

1. if they find work interesting
2. good working conditions (clean, quiet, air conditioned).
3. convenient working hours
4. good holidays
5. useful perks (such as employee discounts or free childcare.)

Q2 Complete the sentences below, using words from the box to fill in the spaces.

> meet people   income   identity
> non-financial   fulfilling

Most people go to work to earn an **income**. Some people choose to do whatever job earns the most money, but others take **non-financial** reasons into account. Nurses and social workers often choose those jobs because they find them **fulfilling**. Some people want to work somewhere where they can **meet people**. Belonging to a particular profession can also give people an **identity**.

Q3 Write out the following words under the correct heading of skills or attributes.

> able to type fast ✓   friendly manner ✓   work well under pressure ✓
> good eye for detail ✓   fluent in a foreign language ✓   able to organise people ✓

Skills	Attributes
able to type fast	friendly manner
fluent in a foreign language	good eye for detail
able to organise people	work well under pressure

I write, therefore I am...

People often define themselves by their job. When you meet someone for the first time they usually mention their job straight away. I'm still not sure if that's really sad or not.

Section Four — People

Employment and the Law

Q1 Which law says that you must receive a written contract within one month of starting your new job?

Employment rights act 1996

Q2 Name the laws that would protect the following people.

a) Someone who feels she has been treated unfairly because she is female.

sex discrimination act 1975

b) Someone who feels he has been unfairly treated because of the colour of his skin.

race relations act 1976

c) Someone who has been treated unfairly because she has an illness which causes her to walk with a limp.

disability discrimination act 2005

Q3 What is the maximum number of hours you are allowed to work in a week?

48 hours

Q4 Which Act is concerned with the lighting, heating and cleanliness of toilets?

The 1961 factories act.

Q5 What law protects workers who need to be at a computer for most of the working day?

The 1992 workplace regulations.

Q6 Which law generally is concerned for the general health and safety of employees?

The health and safety at work act 1974.

Q7 Give two fair reasons why a business may have to get rid of a worker.

a) If they are incapable of doing their job correctly.
b) They have shown gross misconduct

Q8 What is the only reason why an employee can be made redundant from their job?

If the job they are employed to do no longer exists.

Q9 If a person feels they have been unfairly dismissed what can they do about it? What might they hope to achieve by doing this?

appeal to an employment tribunal. They can gain compensation or reinstate the employee

Section Four — People

Motivation Theory

Q1 Maslow believed that workers are motivated by five different factors. Write down a description of what each of the factors is in the spaces below.

FACTORS   DESCRIPTION

a) Self-actualisation   ....
                                  ....

b) Self-esteem   ....
                                  ....

c) Love and belonging   ....
                                  ....

d) Safety   ....
                                  ....

e) Physical survival   ....
                                  ....

Q2 In the box are different needs that workers have. Write them down in the table below — dividing them into hygiene factors and motivating factors.

> rest breaks   promotion opportunites   clean workplace
> praise for work   safe workplace   taking on responsibility

Hygiene factors   Motivating factors

a) ....   a) ....
b) ....   b) ....
c) ....   c) ....

Q3 McGregor believed there were two types of managers. Write a brief description of Theory X managers and Theory Y managers in the spaces below.

Theory X managers ....
....

Theory Y managers ....
....

Section Four — People

2 More Motivation Theories

Q1 Complete the sentences below, using words from the box to fill in the spaces.

> managers earning money promotion twentieth century
> committees efficient time and motion boredom safety risks

Taylor developed his theory at the beginning of the ....

He believed workers were lazy and only interested in ....

He thought bosses should carry out .... studies to find out the

most .... ways to do the different tasks that make up a job. Taylor

thought that each task should be done by different workers and ....

should be appointed to make sure they carried out the work efficiently. In practice, Taylor's

theory didn't always increase productivity because of the ....

for the workers of doing tasks repetitively.

Q2 What did Mayo think helped to motivate workers? Tick the correct answer.

☐ Managers giving workers strict instructions on how tasks should be completed.

☐ Managers taking a personal interest in the workers as people.

☐ Workers organising their own work, without supervision by managers.

Q3 Tick whether the following statement is true or false. If it's false, write the correct version.

Mayo thought it wasn't important for employees to have the same goals as the firm they worked for — they would work hard anyway, in order to get paid.

True ☐   False ☐

....

....

Q4 Write down three different problems with motivation theory as a whole.

a) ....

....

b) ....

....

c) ....

....

Section Four — People

Financial Rewards

Q1 Fill in the table by deciding which is the most appropriate method of payment for each of the jobs and giving your reasons.

time rate ✓   piece rate ✓   salary ✓
commission ✓   bonus time rate ✓   profit sharing ✓

Occupation	Financial Reward	Reasons
Clerk	salary	a fixed amount paid every month. usually paid when not directly helped
Car salesperson	commission	They earn a small basic salary and then earn more for every item they sell
Director of a business (expected to grow rapidly)	bonus time rate	Paid if the worker has met their performance targets
Bricklayer	time rate	paid workers by the hour. e.g. £5 = 1 hour
Car park attendent	profit sharing	each worker has an agreed share of profits. the company does well → payment is bigger
Factory worker (hoped to achieve above a minimum amount each day)	piece rate	10p per buttons sewn on. 10p × 200 = £2000 paid

Q2 Which of the financial rewards in the above table is a fixed amount paid every month?

salary

Q3 Commissions, bonuses and profit-sharing are all examples of which type of pay?

performance related pay

You've just won £500,000 — but we don't want to give you that...

I often get letters through my door telling me that I've won a huge financial reward. Every time I ring the premium rate number and every time I win a £1.50 underlay voucher.

Section Four — People

Non-Financial Motivation

Q1 Job rotation is a method of getting workers to move from one job to another. Give one advantage and one disadvantage of this system.

Advantage: workers don't get so bored, and learn more jobs. They'll be able to cover if someone's ill.

Disadvantage: one boring job is replaced by another boring job. It doesn't help job satisfaction.

Q2 Job enlargement means giving the worker more of the same type of work. Give one advantage and one disadvantage of this system.

Advantage: gives the job greater variety, and their good performance is being recognised.

Disadvantage: The person thinks they are just being given more work, and it can be demotivating.

Q3 Job enrichment means giving more variety of work to the worker leading to more interesting work. Give one advantage and one disadvantage of this system.

Advantage: The worker may become more motivated and work harder.

Disadvantage: They may expect a pay rise as well.

Q4 Complete the following sentences, using words from the box to fill in the spaces.

> motivate ✓   teams ✓   motor industry ✓   productivity ✓
> continuous improvement ✓   quality of work ✓

Kaizen is a Japanese word used often in businesses. It means continuous improvement.
Workers are organised into teams with the responsibility of finding ways to increase productivity and quality of work.
The system aims to motivate workers. In the UK it is used mainly in the motor industry.

Section Four — People

Recruitment — Job Analysis

Q1 Each of the words in the box is a heading from either a job description or a person specification. Write them in the correct column of the table.

> personal qualities   job title   reports to   skills   desirable
> responsible for   essential   duties and responsibilities   main purpose of job

Job Description Headings	Person Specification Headings
....	....
....	....
....	....
....	....
....	....

Q2 Name one way that a firm might fill a vacancy without advertising for the post.

....

....

Q3 Why would only specialist and senior posts be advertised in the national press?

....

....

Q4 Write down three other places where firms could advertise for a post.

a) ....

b) ....

c) ....

Section Four — People

Recruitment — the Selection Process

Q1 Write down three things that might appear on a CV.

1. The persons details
2. qualifications
3. Skills

Q2 Explain the difference between a letter of application and an application form.

An application form tells the firm only what they want to know. A letter is about themselves at length.

Q3 Complete the following sentences, using words from the box to fill in the spaces.

> different ✓   same questions ✓
> panel interviews ✓   unnaturally ✓   fair ✓

Interviews for senior positions are often **panel interviews**. Interviewers should ask the **same questions** to all candidates so the process is **fair**. Some people think that interviews are bad because people behave **different**, and the skills needed to do well in interviews are **unnaturally** from job skills.

Q4 Match up each recruitment tests with the correct description by drawing a straight line.

Test	Description
Skills tests	tell the firm whether the candidate has the right personal qualities
Aptitude tests	tell the firm whether the candidate has the ability to do the job
Personality tests	tell the firm whether the candidate has the potential to learn how to do the job
Group tests	tell the firm whether the candidate has good leadership and decision-making skills

Matches drawn:
- Skills tests → has the ability to do the job
- Aptitude tests → has the potential to learn how to do the job
- Personality tests → has the right personal qualities
- Group tests → good leadership and decision-making skills

Ippy dippy, my blue ship — yep, you're hired...

Lots of companies ask applicants to do a test these days, so it's no longer good enough to be really slick at interviews — you've got to know stuff as well. Rats.

Section Four — People

Staff Training

Q1 Tick the correct box to finish the sentence.

Induction training occurs...

☐ ...throughout a worker's employment.

☐ ...at the beginning of a worker's employment.

☐ ...whenever a new skill needs to be learned.

Q2 Write down one advantage and one disadvantage of learning through on-the-job training.

Advantage: ....

Disadvantage: ....

Q3 Write down one advantage and one disadvantage of learning through off-the-job training.

Advantage: ....

Disadvantage: ....

Q4 Give an explanation of each of these training schemes funded by the government.

a) Learning Skills Councils

....

b) Investors in People

....

c) National Vocational Qualification

....

Q5 Write down a reason why the government wants the workforce to be highly trained.

....

....

Section Four — People

Trade Unions

Q1 Write down six reasons why someone might wish to join a trade union.

i) ....

ii) ....

iii) ....

iv) ....

v) ....

vi) ....

Q2 Give one reason why someone might **not** want to join a trade union.

....

....

Q3 Place the following unions under one of the four headings.

> PFA (Professional Footballers Association)
> UCATT (Union of Craft and Allied Trades Technicians)
> NUM (National Union of Mineworkers)
> EFTU (Engineering and Fastener Trades Union)
> CWU (Communication works union)
> USDAW (Union of shops and Allied Distributive Workers)
> UNISON (Local Government and health care workers – the biggest union)
> NUJ (National Union of Journalists)
> EQUITY (The Actors Union)

Craft Unions	Industrial Unions	General Unions	White Collar Unions
....	....	....	....
....	....	....	....
....	....	....	....
....	....	....	....
....	....	....	....

Section Four — People

Industrial Disputes

Q1 Four options may be open to workers involved in an industrial dispute. Write down the terms described below.

a) Only working normal hours: ....

b) Doing exactly what it says in the workers job description and no more: ....

c) Withdrawal of labour: ....

d) Doing what it says in the workers job description but doing it very slowly: ....

Q2 One possible solution to the threat of a strike is to use the services of ACAS. What do these letters stand for?

....

Q3 If there is stalemate between the workers and managers ACAS may try to get them to start talking to each other. What is this process called?

....

Q4 Decide whether each of these laws favour workers or managers and explain why.

a) The Employment Act 1980

....

b) The Employment Act 1982

....

c) The Trade Union Act 1984

....

d) The Employment Act 1988

....

e) The Employment Relations Act 1999

....

We've never had an industrial dispute — oh yes we have...

There are never any disputes in the CGP offices. Except that time when Katherine stole my blue pen. She tried to put it back on my desk but I could tell that some ink had been used. So I went on strike.

Section Four — People

Section Five — Finance

Business Costs

Q1 Fill in the missing words in the following paragraph about direct and indirect costs, using the words below.

direct costs are those costs which are directly used in making the items. **indirect** costs are not used directly in making the goods but are still important in getting the items to the **customer**. Increases in these costs will affect the amount of **profit** made so businesses need to **control** them and understand any increase or decrease in them. Businesses need to find ways to **monitor** these cost increases to make a profit.

~~customer   control   direct   indirect   profit   monitor~~

Q2 Put the factors in the box in the correct column of the table to show whether each is a fixed or a variable cost.

~~factory labour   management salaries   office rent   machinery   raw materials   telephone bills~~

Fixed cost	Variable cost
office rent	factory labour
telephone bills	machinery
management salaries	raw materials

Q3 Write 'average cost' or 'marginal cost' next to each of these definitions.

a) This tells the company how much it will cost to make one more product — it's the cost of increasing output by one unit. **marginal cost**

b) This is how much each product cost to make. It can be found by dividing total cost by output. **average cost**

Break-even Analysis

Q1 Fill in the gaps in the following paragraph using the list below.

The break-even point (BEP) is a position where total .... are equal to total .... At this position a business is neither making a .... nor a .... The selling price minus the .... gives the contribution per unit. The BEP is found by dividing .... costs (costs which do not vary with how much is produced) by the .... per unit. BEP is the minimum number of .... needed to break even.

> fixed   revenue   items   variable costs   profit   contribution   loss   costs

Q2 Answer the following questions using the information in the box below.

> A business has a production capacity of 5000 items. Fixed costs are £10000. Items are sold for £10 each. Variable costs are £6 per item.

a) From this information, calculate the BEP.

BEP: .... = ... items

b) Profit is found by multiplying contribution per unit by the number of items sold after BEP. Using this, find the profit if the business sells:

i) 2501 items: ....

ii) 3217 items: ....

iii) 4716 items: ....

iv) 4999 items: ....

c) How much will the business lose if it only sells 2488 items? ....

d) If all the other costs and selling price remained the same but the fixed costs increased to £15000, work out the new BEP.

BEP: .... = ... items

e) If, instead, only the selling price had to be changed to £12 per item, and all the other costs did not change at all, work out the BEP.

BEP: .... = ... items

I can break even the sturdiest of chairs...

If a company breaks even, it covers all of its costs. If it sells more it'll make a profit, which is always the name of the game. The tricky bit is working the break-even value out each time.

Section Five — Finance

Internal Sources of Finance

Q1 Fill in the missing words in the following paragraph about direct and indirect costs, using the words below.

> delay payment   expanding   start-up capital
> liquidity shortfall   assets   suppliers   working capital

Every business, large or small, needs to have **start-up capital** to begin and then have enough **working capital** to meet the day-to-day running of the business. This money is used to buy different items which are called **assets**. The business needs to arrange to purchase items from their **suppliers** so that customers will be able to buy them. Not all customers will pay in cash but will **delay payment** (this is called paying on credit). All businesses need to monitor cash-flow to make sure they do not have a **liquidity shortfall**. Some of these funds can be used for **expanding** the business so that it can grow to its full potential (called economies of scale).

Q2 Fill in the table with benefits and problems of the following internal sources of finance.

Source of finance	Benefits	Problems
Retained profits	profits that th	
Credit control		
Fixed Assets		
Run down stocks		
Re-invest savings		

External Sources of Finance

Q1 Name two sources of external finance that might be useful to someone intending to trade sports equipment on a market stall.

a) personal savings

b) friends or family

Q2 Name four major problems there may be in trying to arrange enough finance to start-up the sports equipment stall.

a) Amount of money needed

b) Length of time

c) Cost of the finance

d) Size and type of company

Q3 Fill in the table with benefits and problems of the following external sources of finance.

Source of finance	Benefits	Problems
Overdraft	lets the firm take more money out of bank	Interest charges are high.
Late payment of bills	holding onto money that they owe.	annoy the firm they're doing bussiness with
Bank loan	quick and easy	repaying interest
Fixed assets lease	less initial finance is needed to obtain the asset	overtime works out to be more experiance.
Hire purchase	It buys the assets in instalments.	interest payment can be very high.
Share issue	does not have to be repaid to shareholders	more shares mean less control

Section Five — Finance

Budgeting

Q1 Fill in the missing words in the paragraph using the list below.

All good businesses try to plan .... Their most important area of concern is how much money they can expect to spend and receive in the future. All businesses need to .... what they believe will happen. Suppose .... shows that yo-yos are likely to be the new trend. Businesses need to plan and make sure that there are enough yo-yos made to meet .... The business must start making these yo-yos months before the summer. The business will need to make sure that they have the .... and enough ....

> research   employees   demand   ahead   materials   predict

Q2 Decide whether the following examples are **favourable** or **unfavourable**.

a) If revenue is lower than planned this is ....
b) If revenue turns out to be better than planned it is said to be ....
c) If expenditure (money spent) is more than you planned it is ....
d) If expenditure is lower than you planned it is said to be ....

Q3 Now complete the November budget for Yummo Chocolate Ltd by filling in the gaps in the table.

	Forecast	Actual	Variance	Favourable or unfavourable?
Sales revenue	25,000	29,600		
Raw Materials	16,000	14,700		
Wages	8,000	9,800		
Telephone	200	200		
Petrol	600	500		
Electricity	120	160		
Total expenditure				
Profit/loss				

Section Five — Finance

Cash Flow

At the beginning of September, you have £10 saved. You receive £15 per week pocket money. You have a morning newspaper round that pays £5 per round (£7 on Sundays), and an evening paper round that pays £4 for each round Monday to Saturday.

Earnings:
Week 1: Morning paper round Monday to Saturday.
Week 2: Evening paper round Monday to Thursday.
Week 3: Morning paper round Monday to Thursday
Week 4: Evening paper round Monday to Saturday, and the morning round on Sunday.

Spending:
£2 a day for buses on weekdays.
£3 a day at school.
£15 on a CD each Saturday.
During week 2 you also have to buy your sister a birthday present for £5.

Q1 Complete the cash flow table below using the information above.

	Week 1	Week 2	Week 3	Week 4
INCOME:	10	15	29	34
Pocket money	15	15	15	15
Paper round	30	16	20	31
Total cash inflow	45	31	35	46
PAYMENTS:	40	45	40	40
Bus fares	10	10	10	10
School money	15	15	15	15
CDs	15	15	15	15
Present	0	5	0	0
Total payments	40	45	40	40
Balance at start of month	10	15	29	34
Balance at end of month	15	29	34	40

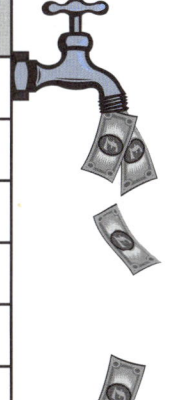

Q2 In which week does a problem occur? Suggest a way of avoiding the problem.

....

....

My cash always flows straight down the drain...

...every payday I go straight out and buy all of the mange tout peas I can find, and then I cook a massive stir fry which I can't eat. I wish I'd learn my lesson. Mmm — payday tomorrow... peas...

Section Five — Finance

The Trading, Profit and Loss Account

Q1 Write down whether these definitions are gross profit or net profit.

.... is found by looking at the amount of trade a business has had over the year. It is found by subtracting the total purchases from the total sales.

.... is found by taking all the expenses or overheads that have been used in the year away from the gross profit.

Q2 Using the information below, complete the trading, profit and loss account.

J. Bollingblow Enterprises was set up on 1st January 1996 and sells CDs. When the business was set up the owner bought in 100 CDs at a cost of £10 each.

During the course of the year the owner bought a further 500 CDs also for £10 each.

The CDs were sold for cash at £15 each. The owner pays wages of £20 a day for 50 Saturdays of the year. By 31st December 1996 the owner had 200 CDs left in stock.

Trading account for J. Bollingblow Enterprises		£
Turnover		....
Cost of sales:		
Opening stock	....	
Purchases	....	
Total	....	
Closing stock	....	
Cost of sales		....
Gross profit		....

Profit and loss account for J. Bollingblow Enterprises		£
Expenses/Overheads:		
Rent for market stall	500	
Mail costs	300	
Advertising	120	
Wages for the year	....	
Total expenses for year		....
Net profit		....

Section Five — Finance

The Balance Sheet — Net Assets

Q1 A sole trader who has been trading for one year must now produce a balance sheet for the Bank Manager. Prepare her balance sheet using the information below.

Capital	£800.00
Machinery	£284.00
Debtors	£351.70
Bank Overdraft	£104.88
Cash in hand	£211.88
Van	£450.00
Creditors	£324.25
Stock at end of period	£115.00
Net Profit	£153.45
Debentures	£30.00

BALANCE SHEET   E. BLYTON – TIMBER TRADING, December 31, 2001

Fixed Assets   £

    Machinery   ....

    Van   ....

    ....

Current Assets

    Stock at December 31, 2000   ....

    Debtors   ....

    Cash in hand   ....

    ....

Current Liabilities

    Creditors   ....

    Bank Overdraft   ....

Working Capital   ....

Net Assets   ....

Financed by

    Owners Capital   ....

    Net Profit   ....

    ....

Debentures   ....

Capital Employed   ....

Section Five — Finance

The Balance Sheet — Capital Employed

Q1 Fill in the missing words in the following paragraph using the list below.

> net profit   bank loan   long-term liabilities
> capital employed   balance   capital   shareholders funds   net assets

.... are the items which the business owes to others but does not expect to pay them back for more than one year. One of the most common types is called a .... which means the business borrows a sum of money for a fixed period of time.

.... — this section says where all the money has come from to pay for these assets. This includes the amount of .... put into the business and any profit made during the year (.................................. only) will be added to this.

The balance sheet must .... — the fixed assets are added to the current assets and the current and long term liabilities are taken away from these assets. This gives a heading called .... The 'financed by' section must be added together and this total is called ....

Q2 What is the name of the law which says that annual accounts have to be produced by limited companies?

....

Q3 How much do the accounts cost for anyone wishing to see them?

....

Q4 Why might the government be interested in seeing these accounts?

....

Can't... write... too... busy... balancing...

The first thing to learn is <u>why</u> it's called a balance sheet. You need to know everything on the last two pages in real detail — balance sheets almost always crop up in exams.

Section Five — Finance

Analysis of Accounts — Ratios

Q1 Using the information below, work out the gross profit margin for 2000 and 2001.

> 2000: sales £20,000, gross profit £7,000
> 2001: sales £30,000, gross profit £9,000

2000 gross profit margin = ... %

2001 gross profit margin = ... %

Q2 Using the information below, work out the net profit margin for 2000 and 2001.

> 2000: sales £60,000, net profit £8,000
> 2001: sales £50,000, net profit £7,000

2000 net profit margin = ... %

2001 net profit margin = ... %

Q3 Using the information below, work out the return on capital employed (ROCE) for 2000 and 2001.

> 2000: net profit £11,000
> 2001: net profit £18,000
> £100,000 capital employed in 2000 and £200,000 capital employed in 2001.

ROCE 2000 = ... %

ROCE 2001 = ... %

Q4 Using the information below, work out the current ratio for 2000 and 2001.

> 2000: current assets £16,000
> 2001: current assets £10,000
> £12,000 current liabilities in 2000 and £9,500 current liabilities in 2001.

2000 current ratio = ... %

2001 current ratio = ... %

Q5 Using the information below, work out the acid test ratio for 2000 and 2001.

> 2000: bank £16,000, debtors £4,500
> 2001: bank £2,500, debtors £22,000
> 2000 current liabilities £30,750, 2001 current liabilities £21,000.

2000 acid test ratio = ... %

2001 acid test ratio = ... %

Section Five — Finance

Using Ratios

B. BEYTON — TRADING, PROFIT AND LOSS ACCOUNT	£
Sales	50000
Purchases	30000
Gross profit	20000
Expenses	18000
Net profit	2000

B. BEYTON — BALANCE SHEET		£
Fixed Assets		
Premises		6900
Machinery		2500
Van		3200
		12600
Current Assets		
Stock	1560	
Debtors	5500	
Cash in hand	300	
	7360	
Current Liabilities		
Creditors	1700	
Working Capital		5660
Net Assets		18260
Financed by		
Owners Capital		18000
Net Profit		2000
Bank overdraft		60
		20060
Drawings		1800
Capital Employed		18260

Net profits low again this year.
Note to self: Buy a bigger net.

Q1 Use the above information to work out the following margins.

a) Gross profit margin = ... %   d) Current ratio = ... %

b) Net profit margin = ... %   e) Acid test ratio = ... %

c) ROCE = ... %

Q2 Comment on the ratios for B. Beyton and highlight any concerns and suggestions for this business.

....
....
....
....
....

Current ratio — too many sultanas...

If you're having troubling figuring out how to calculate each type of ratio, look over page 47 again and then come back to this one. This stuff is difficult but we both know you can get it figured out.

Section Five — Finance

Section Six — Growth of Firms

Starting a New Business

Q1 Write down THREE reasons why people start their own business. Write your answers in the spaces below.

1. *Some people enjoy the independance*

2. *The owner has a new idea or product*

3. *To help other people.*

Q2 Complete the sentences using some of the words below to fill in the spaces.

> ~~income~~   ~~vary~~   ~~delegate~~   ~~subordinates~~
> ~~responsibility~~   ~~profit~~   ~~very long hours~~

There are problems with running your own business. The business may take time to produce a *profit* and so the owner's *income* may be small and *vary* from week to week. There is no one else to take the blame if things go wrong – the owner must be prepared to take *responsibility*. Owners of new firms generally work *very long hours*. As the business grows the owner needs to learn to *delegate* responsibility to *subordinates*.

Q3 Which of the following is NOT an essential personal characteristic of a good business person? Tick the correct answer.

- [ ] Must be resourceful and independent
- [ ] Must be self-motivated and have a desire to succeed
- [x] Must have a large sum of money to invest in the business

I would be self-motivated — but I can't be bothered...

Most of this stuff is just common sense, unlike lots of Business Studies, which is mostly nonsense. New businesses are set up in this country all the time, so you really need to know about them.

The Business Plan

Q1 Complete the sentences using some of the words below to fill in the spaces.

> ~~time and money~~   ~~resources~~   ~~start-up capital~~ ~~venture capitalists~~
> ~~planning stage~~   ~~owner~~   ~~banks~~   ~~sound investment~~

It is important that the **owner** thinks carefully what the business is going to do and what **resources** are needed. This will help calculate how much **start-up capital** is needed to finance the business. It is unlikely that the owner will have enough money to start the business. Financial backers such as **venture capitalists** or **banks** will need to be convinced that the new business is a **sound investment**. The hope is that if the business is a bad idea, either the owner or the financial backer will realise this at the **planning stage** before they have wasted lots of **time and money** on a business that was never going to work.

Q2 A Business Plan should contain a number of different sections. Write down a description of each section in the spaces below.

a) Personal Details **of the owner and other important personnel - like their CVs.**

b) Mission Statement **a poncey way of describing the broad aims of the company.**

c) Objectives **These are more concrete and specific aims.**

d) Product Description **including details of the market and competitors**

e) Production Details **how the firm will makes its product or provides its service.**

f) Staffing Requirements **how many people, their job descriptions and the expected wage bill**

g) Finance **It should explain how much money is needed to start up the business.**

Section Six — Growth of Firms

Starting a Business — Help and Support

Q1 Write down TWO ways that the government can benefit if more people start their own business.

a) Reduces ....

....

b) ....

....

Q2 Which of the following is a government agency which provides help and support to new businesses? Tick the correct answer.

☐ Learning and Skills Council

☐ Venture Capital

☐ Multinational Enterprise

Q3 Complete the sentences using some of the words below to fill in the spaces.

> profit   bankrupt   banks   account   reduce the chances
> business advisors   private   competitors   money

Some firms in the .... sector aim to make a .... by providing help and support to new businesses. The most obvious examples are .... They publish guides on how to write a business plan and have .... who will talk with potential entrepreneurs. They do this for two main reasons. Firstly, to get the business to open an .... with them and not with one of their .... and secondly, to .... of the new business becoming .... and owing the bank lots of ....

Q4 Tick whether the following statement is true or false. If it's false write the correct version.

> The Prince's Youth Trust was set up when the Prince of Wales realised there were limited employment opportunities for elderly people living in rural areas.

True ☐   False ☐

....

....

Section Six — Growth of Firms

Growth of Firms — Internal Expansion

Q1 There are four main reasons why a business will want to expand. Write a description of each reason in the spaces below.

a) Economies of Scale ....

b) Diversification ....

c) Financial Support ....

d) Personal Vanity ....

Q2 Which of the following is NOT an example of internal expansion? Tick the correct answer.

☐ Producing more of the same product to sell in existing markets.

☐ Buying a competitor and selling its products in a new market.

☐ Producing a new product and selling it in existing markets.

Ben could feel the internal expansion happening already.

Q3 Explain the difference between line extension and diversification. Write your answer in the space below.

....

Q4 Write down one benefit and one drawback of internal expansion.

Advantage ....

Drawback ....

Go go gadget internal expansion...

The four main reasons for internal expansion are the key points on this page. Oh, and make extra sure that you remember that internal expansion is all about firms expanding their own activities.

Section Six — Growth of Firms

Growth of Firms — Takeovers and Mergers

Q1 Tick whether the following statement is true or false. If it's false write the correct version.

> A merger is when two firms agree to join together.
> A takeover is when one firm buys another.

True ☐   False ☐

....

....

Q2 In the box are different ways that one firm can join with another. Write them down in the table alongside the correct heading.

> when two firms with nothing in common join together
> when a firm joins with a supplier   when two competitors join together
> when a firm joins with a customer

Type of integration	Description
Horizontal integration	....
Forward vertical integration	....
Backward vertical integration	....
Lateral / conglomerate integration	....

Q3 Complete the sentences using some of the words below to fill in the spaces.

> redundant   culture   tension and uncertainty
> hostile   management styles   motivated

It is very hard to make two different businesses work as one. ....
are often different in the two firms – the employees of one may be used to one company
.... and not be .... by the style used
in the other. Takeovers can create bad feeling. Often a firm agrees to be taken over, but
sometimes the takeover is .... and unpopular. Mergers usually
lead to cost-cutting by making people .... This leads to
.... among workers.

Section Six — Growth of Firms

Effects of Expansion — Economies of Scale

Q1 Tick whether the following statement is true or false. If it's false write the correct version.

> Economies of scale are the reduction in total cost that results from operating a business on a larger scale.

True ☐   False ☐

....
....

Q2 There are six main economies of scale. Write a description of each one in the spaces below.

a) Purchasing economies ....
....

b) Marketing economies ....
....

c) Managerial economies ....
....

d) Financial economies ....
....

e) Technical economies ....
....

f) Risk-bearing economies ....
....

Q3 Write down a description of two external economies of scale in the space below.

1 ....
....
....

2 ....
....
....

Section Six — Growth of Firms

Effects of Expansion — Communication

Q1 Tick whether the following statement is true or false. If it's false write the correct version.

> Effective communication requires feedback to confirm that the message has been understood.

True ☐   False ☐

....

....

Q2 Complete the table by writing down one benefit and one drawback of each communication medium.

Type of communication	Benefit	Drawback
Written		
Verbal		
Visual		

Q3 Complete the sentences using some of the words below to fill in the spaces.

> orders   low morale   customers and suppliers
> poor decisions   not being listened to   confidence

Poor internal communication can result in .... and .... if people feel that they are .... Poor external communication can result in .... losing .... in the company — this can result in fewer ....

Am I making myself clear?   Hello... Is anyone there...?
If a large firm has a breakdown in communication it can cause massive problems.
Here at CGP we communicate with messages attached to the backs of trained postal gerbils.

Section Six — Growth of Firms

Communication — Networks and Hierarchies

Q1 Look at the diagram on the right. How long is the chain of command in Clevercloggs Software? Tick the correct answer.

☐ 3   ☐ 6   ☐ 12

Clevercloggs Software Ltd.
I. Givordas
Director
↓
I. M. Busy
Manager

Worker 1, Worker 2, Worker 3, Worker 4, Worker 5, Worker 6, Worker 7, Worker 8, Worker 9

Q2 Write down one drawback of a wide span of control.

....
....
....

Q3 Draw a diagram in the box below to illustrate a wheel network connecting nine people.

Q4 Write down one benefit and one drawback of a connected network.

Benefit ....
....
Drawback ....
....

Section Six — Growth of Firms

Multinational Firms

Q1 Write down three benefits of being a multinational firm.

1 ....
....

2 ....
....

3 ....
....

Q2 Complete the sentences using some of the words below to fill in the spaces.

> employment   balance of payments   foreign technology
> export revenue   working methods   taxation   foreign investment

Multinational Enterprises (MNEs) are often a source of ....

money and create .... for local people. MNEs bring their own

methods of working, giving the host country access to .... and

....

The profits of the MNE can be a source of .... revenue for the

host country's government. .... from MNE sales abroad can

improve the country's ....

Q3 Write down three problems that MNEs can cause in the host countries where they operate.

1 ....
....

2 ....
....

3 ....
....

Section Six — Growth of Firms

Competition and Monopoly

Q1 Tick whether the following statement is true or false. If it's false write the correct version.

> A competitive market is one where there are a small number of producers selling to a large number of consumers.

True ☐   False ☐

....

....

Q2 Write down in the space below one benefit to consumers of a competitive market.

....

....

Q3 Why are prices generally higher in monopoly markets than in competitive markets? Tick the correct answer.

☐ Consumers know that products made in monopoly markets are of better quality.

☐ Consumers in monopoly markets are richer and so can afford the higher prices.

☐ The consumer has less choice and so has to pay the higher prices.

Q4 Complete the sentences using some of the words below to fill in the spaces.

> research and development   higher prices   same product
> low prices   standard of living   less money

Competition is fine if it delivers .... But sometimes all the firms end up making the .... This results in fewer different products for the consumer. If each firm makes fewer profits there may be .... available to develop new and better products.

Monopolies generally result in .... and so consumers end up with a lower .... But the high profits can be spent on the .... of new products.

Section Six — Growth of Firms

The Survival of Small Firms

Q1 Write down in the spaces below three reasons why some small firms remain small.

1 ....
....

2 ....
....

3 ....
....

Q2 Complete the sentences using some of the words below to fill in the spaces.

> gap   customers   niche   needs   personal service

Small firms have a number of advantages over larger firms. They can get to know their

.... individually and so offer a more .... As a

result they can be more responsive to individual customer .... The firm

can be set up to exploit a .... in the market; small firms are often more

able to supply .... products than large firms.

Q3 Which of the following is a benefit to the economy of small firms? Tick the correct answer.

☐ Small firms help the economy to exploit gaps in the market.
   This forces larger firms to remain competitive.

☐ Small firms benefit more from economies of scale than larger firms.

☐ Small firms are able to take advantage of risk bearing economies of scale.

Q4 Why are small firms likely to employ people on part-time or temporary contracts?

....
....
....

Small is beautiful...
Not every firm has the ambition to become a sprawling mega-company, and even if they wanted to most firms stay small anyway. You need to know the benefits and disadvantages of small firms.

Section Six — Growth of Firms

Business Failure

Q1 What happens when a firm becomes insolvent? Tick the correct answer.

☐ The firm doesn't have enough working capital to pay its short term liabilities

☐ The firm doesn't have enough short term liabilities to pay its working capital

☐ The firm doesn't have enough profit to pay its cash flow

Q2 Write down an explanation of why overtrading can be a cause of cash-flow problems.

....

....

Q3 Complete the sentences using some of the words below to fill in the spaces.

> official receiver   assets   full legal rights   going concern
> bankrupt   personal property   debts   creditor

If a firm has a cash flow problem it might not be able to pay its debts.

A .... might sue the firm in court to try and get its money back. If the firm does not have enough cash to pay them the court may appoint an

.... to run the business. The official receiver has

.... over all of the owner's ....

The first concern is to find the funds needed to pay the firm's

.... If the official receiver believes that the firm can still be

profitable it will be run as a .... If not then the owner's

.... will be sold to pay the firm's debts, the firm will close and

the owner will be declared ....

Q4 Tick whether the following statement is true or false. If it's false write the correct version.

> When a Public Limited Company (PLC) goes into liquidation its assets are sold and the money is used to pay the firm's creditors.

True ☐   False ☐

....

....

Section Six — Growth of Firms

Section Seven — External Influences

The Business Cycle

Q1 Complete the sentences below, using the words from the box to fill in the spaces.

> total income   annual percentage change
> Gross Domestic Product   total output

.... measures the .... of the economy, which is calculated by adding together the amount produced by all UK firms.

GDP can also be measured by calculating the .... of firms in the UK economy. Economic growth is defined as the

.... in GDP.

Q2 Write TRUE or FALSE after the following statements about economic growth.

a) Economic growth means everyone has improved living standards and a better quality of life.   ....

b) In times of economic growth some groups of society benefit but others can lose out.   ....

c) An increase in GDP can often lead to an increase in pollution. ....

d) Growth rates in the UK have stayed the same over the past twenty years.   ....

e) In the early 1980s and early 1990s the United Kingdom experienced periods of negative economic growth. ....

Q3 On the diagram below draw the regular pattern of the business cycle. Label your business cycle to show booms and recessions.

Economic growth ↑

→ Time

Unemployment and Inflation

Q1 Complete the sentences using the words below to fill in the spaces.

> rise   inflation   unemployed   fall   recession   boom

Somebody is .... if they are looking for a job but cannot find one.

Unemployment falls in a .... and rises in a ....

A general increase in the level of prices is called .... Prices usually

.... in a boom and .... in a recession.

Q2 Give one way in which unemployment causes a problem for:

a) the government

....

b) firms

....

c) individuals

....

Q3 Explain each of the following statements about inflation.

a) "Inflation creates uncertainty for firms."

....

....

b) "The UK's inflation rate has varied over the past twenty years."

....

....

c) "If the inflation rate in the UK is higher than
other countries it can cause problems for our firms."

....

....

Government Spending and Taxation

Q1 Complete the sentences using the words below to fill in the spaces.

> education   recession   demand   social security

Government spending goes up in a .... The government will spend more on .... because there will be more people unemployed. This accounted for most of the government spending in 2000-2001. Next were health, ... , defence and law and order. Government spending helps to maintain .... for the economy's businesses.

Q2 The table below gives three areas of government spending. Write out the words from the box into the right place.

> defence industry   medical companies   construction firms

Government spending	People who will benefit
Building new roads	....
Buying new fighter planes	....
Improving the health service	....

Q3 Draw a straight line from each tax to its definition.

Corporation Tax

Income Tax

Council Tax

National Insurance

Value Added Tax

Pays for the Jobs Seekers Allowance

Paid to the local council for services including the library and waste management

A tax paid on earnings

A tax on the firm's profits

17.5% added to most purchases

Section Seven — External Influences

Government Economic Policy

Q1 Write TRUE or FALSE after the following statements about fiscal policy.

a) Greater spending in the economy can be created by reducing taxes and increasing government spending. ....

b) If the government wishes to reduce inflation it will reduce taxes and increase spending. ....

c) Expansionary fiscal policy involves reducing taxes and increasing government spending. ....

Q2 Complete the sentences using the words below to fill in the spaces.

> unemployment   cheaper   less   demand   inflation   high

When interest rates are .... it is better to save than to borrow. This means that firms and consumers are spending .... This will cause unemployment as firms need fewer workers when .... is decreasing.

When interest rates are low it becomes .... to borrow and you get less interest if you decide to save money in a bank. This encourages firms and consumers to spend more. Just like cutting taxes this can increase demand in the economy and therefore reduce .... Unfortunately this can also lead to ....

Q3 Explain how higher interest rates in the UK affect:

a) savers from abroad
....

b) foreign consumers buying exported goods from the UK
....

c) UK consumers buying imports.
....

d) UK manufacturing firms
....

Government Policy — Consumer Protection

Q1 Complete the table using two of the phrases in the box.

> Competition Commission   Competition Act   Office of Fair Trading

Government body	Role
....	Investigates alleged monopolies. Has the power to fine companies.
....	Can recommend to the government that a monopoly should be broken up into smaller companies.

Q2 Below is a series of customer complaints. Match the complaint with the correct consumer protection law given in the box.

> Weights and Measures Act (1979)   Consumer Credit Act (1974)
> Trade Descriptions Act (1968)   Supply of Goods and Services Act (1982)

Customer complaint	Description
The stitching has come undone on a brand new pair of trainers.	....
A customer has changed her mind after signing a credit agreement to purchase double glazing the day before. The salesman says it's too late because the contract has been signed.	....
A man bought a jacket advertised as waterproof, only to get soaked when it rained.	....
A woman bought a box of cat biscuits. When she opened the box she saw that the box was half full.	....

Dear CGP, I am writing to complain...

...I was horrified to find that your Key Stage 4 'Guide to Armadillo Polishing' left a salty taste in my mouth. I seasoned it with tarragon and yet it still tasted awful. Yours sincerely, Anne Imbecile.

Section Seven — External Influences

Regional Policy

Q1 Complete the sentences using some of the words below to fill in the spaces.

> decline   support   government   structural
> regional   Intermediate   Development   jobs

The government tries to encourage firms to locate themselves in assisted areas. These areas are full of people who want .... but cannot find them. .... Areas receive the most .... from the government. Due to the .... of traditional industries, such as mining, these areas have high levels of .... unemployment. Areas that still need government support, but not as much as Development Areas, are called .... Areas.

Q2 Match the regional aids to their correct description.

> Government Offices   Regional Development Areas
> Regional Enterprise Grants   Regional Selective Assistance   Enterprise Zones

Type of Regional Aid	Description
....	Set up to encourage companies from outside an area to invest in it.
....	A grant for projects that will safeguard or create jobs.
....	Small areas where firms pay less tax and have to comply with fewer government regulations.
....	Government run organisations that are located in assisted areas. The DVLA in Swansea is an example.
....	Given to smaller companies in Development Areas when they are investing in projects that will create jobs.

Q3 Write down one good effect and one bad effect on businesses of regional policy.

Good effect: ....
....

Bad effect: ....
....

Section Seven — External Influences

Non-government Influences on Business

Q1 Match up each pressure group to the correct description by drawing a straight line.

- Greenpeace
- Which?
- www.corpwatch.org
- ASH

- spreads information for anti-corporate protestors
- informs people about which products offer the best value for money
- helped to persuade the government to pass a law making tobacco advertising illegal
- publicises the actions of firms that harm the environment

Q2 Write down what the initials below stand for, and give a brief description of the pressure groups.

ASA: ....

....

BSI: ....

....

Q3 Complete the sentences using the words in the box to fill in the spaces.

> boycott greenwashing profits sales
> the media increase costs public opinion

Bad publicity for a firm can lead to a consumer .... of their products, which

reduces .... and .... On the other hand,

complying with the demands of pressure groups can ....

Large companies are learning to use .... to influence

.... Some firms convince people that they are environmentally friendly

when they are not — this is called ....

Section Seven — External Influences

International Trade

Q1 Give three reasons why international trade happens.

1 ....
....

2 ....
....

3 ....
....

Q2 Complete the table with two benefits and two problems of international trade.

Benefits of International Trade	Problems of International Trade
....	....
....	....

Q3 Complete the sentences using the words below to fill in the spaces.

> communicate needs reduce safety standards
> not pay translated documentation restrictions

A successful exporter needs to understand the .... of the local market and

needs to .... with local customers. Sales brochures may need to be

.... so that local customers understand them.

The foreign exchange risk refers to the risk that the foreign customer will ....

and that the foreign government may put .... on trade. The World Trade

Organisation is also trying to .... to reduce the amount of

.... businesses need to trade internationally.

Exchange Rates

Q1 Write down four reasons why a person or bank in the USA might buy pounds sterling.

1 ....
....

2 ....
....

3 ....
....

4 ....
....

Q2 What effect would US banks buying pounds sterling have on the pound?

....

Q3 Tick whether the following statement is true or false.
If it's false write the correct version.

> The strong pound means that UK firms will earn higher profits, but imported raw materials are more expensive.

True ☐   False ☐

....
....

Q4 Briefly explain the effect of a weak pound on exporters and importers.

....
....
....

Reducing safety standards — an unusual solution...

This stuff is important, but it ain't half dull. When your exams are over, exchange some pounds for euros and hop it to a nice beach, go swimming, go out, get wallpapered, forget this madness...

Section Seven — External Influences

International Trade Restrictions

Q1 Write down four reasons why a government might place restrictions on imports.

1 ....

2 ....

3 ....

4 ....

Q2 Fill in the missing phrases in this table about types of restriction available to governments.

Type of restriction	Description
....	Physical limits placed on the quantity of a product that can be imported
....	Taxes placed in imported products
Subsidies	....
Product safety standards	....
....	The government buying from domestic producers rather than foreign firms

Q3 Complete the sentences using some of the words below to fill in the spaces.

> safety standards   pay higher prices   increase profits
> import restrictions   inefficient   domestic jobs

In theory, reducing foreign competition helps .... for domestic producers and protect .... In practice, other countries retaliate by imposing .... too. One benefit of reducing foreign competition is maintaining .... One big problem is that by restricting efficient foreign competitors, governments protect .... domestic producers. Consumers also have to ....

Section Seven — External Influences

The European Union

Q1 Complete the sentences using some of the words below to fill in the spaces.

> Denmark   1973   Germany   Sweden
> 1958   the Netherlands   1995

The European Union was formed in ....

The founder countries were Belgium, France, Italy, Luxembourg,

.... and ....

The United Kingdom joined the EU in ....

Special offers on Swiss prawns, German paella and Italian bacon butties

Q2 Write a brief explanation of the benefits of the European single market.

....
....
....

Q3 Give two reasons why the single market is not yet a reality.

1 ....
2 ....

Q4 Tick whether the following statement is true or false.
If it's false write the correct version.

> The single market would increase competition between companies, which would result in lower prices and more innovation.

True ☐   False ☐

....
....

Section Seven — External Influences

The Single Currency and EU Laws

Q1 Name the four EU member countries that did <u>not</u> adopt the single currency in 1999.

1 .... 2 ....

3 .... 4 ....

Q2 Write two advantages and two disadvantages of the single currency into the table.

Advantages	Disadvantages
....	....
....	....

Q3 Complete the sentences using some of the words below to fill in the spaces.

> 40 hours   labelling   48 hours   advertising
>
> equal rights   mergers   protect the rights

The European Social Charter is a set of rules designed to .... of employees in the EU. As a result there are .... for part-time and full-time employees. The maximum working week for most workers is

....

The EU competition policy means that all .... of large EU firms must be approved by the EU.

The food industry faces tough .... laws which specify which ingredients should be in certain foods.

EU Laws — look a bit bored, obey the sheepdog...

The section is over — with no rants, nose bleeds, sarcasm, tea-stains or bite marks in the pages. Crumbs. Oh well, here goes — in the nicest possible way — *bring me a peeled grape.* <u>NOW</u>.

Section Seven — External Influences

Section Eight — Business and Change

Deindustrialisation

Q1 What is a correct definition of deindustrialisation? Tick the correct answer.

☐ The building of more factories for manufacturing products.

☐ A declining manufacturing sector along with an increasing service sector.

☐ A declining service sector along with an increasing manufacturing sector.

Q2 Write down three possible reasons why the UK has exported fewer manufactured goods and has imported more of them in the last 50 years.

a) ....

....

....

b) ....

....

....

c) ....

....

....

Q3 Complete the following sentences, using words from the box to fill in the spaces.

> multiplier effect   structural unemployment
>
> regional policy   less money   traditional manufacturing industries

Deindustrialisation has led to the decline of Britain's ....

These areas have suffered increases in .... Local people have

.... to spend, so local businesses have to make people

redundant. This is called the ....

The government may try to help affected areas using ....

Supply-Side Policies

Q1 What is the aim of supply-side policies? Tick the correct answer.

☐ To make British firms more efficient and competitive.

☐ To decrease competition in British firms.

☐ To ensure steady supplies of raw materials for British industries.

Q2 Complete the following sentences, using words from the box to fill in the spaces.

> government   shareholders
> privatised   make a profit   competition

In the 1980s and 1990s, many British industries were .... — they were sold back to private sector shareholders. The government hoped that this would increase .... It was also hoped that the firms would be better run if they were accountable to the .... instead of to the .... The main aim of these firms was now to ....

Q3 Give two examples of industries where the government has lifted restrictions that limit competition between firms.

a) ....

b) ....

Q4 What is the name for the government's lifting of competition restrictions?

....

Section Eight — Business and Change

Flexible Working

Q1 Why might someone prefer to work part-time instead of full-time? Tick the right answer.

☐ Wanting to work more hours each week.

☐ Wanting more income.

☐ Wanting to spend more time with family.

Q2 Name the document that gives equal employment rights to part time and full time workers.

....

Q3 Write down one difference between permanent contracts and temporary contracts.

....

....

....

Q4 Write down an advantage of temporary contracts, from an employer's point of view.

....

....

....

Q5 What is the definition of an enterprise culture? Tick the correct answer.

☐ People wanting to become full time employees for large corporations.

☐ People taking risks and setting up their own businesses.

☐ People going to Star Trek conventions.

CGP — your flexible friend...

My manager's not too much in favour of flexible working. I suggested that I could just come to work when I felt like it, but he didn't see the positive side. It was worth a try though.

Section Eight — Business and Change

New Technology — In The Workplace

Q1 What do CAD and CAM stand for? Write your answer in the space below.

CAD: ....

CAM: ....

Q2 Give two benefits of CAD/CAM in industry.

a) ....

....

b) ....

....

Q3 Complete the following sentences, using words from the box to fill in the spaces.

> email   word processing software   spreadsheets
>
> intranet   desktop publishing software

New computer technology has affected the way offices work. Writing is made quicker by using .... and .... Accounting records can be kept using .... Companies can communicate with customers via .... Communication within the company can be achieved using an ....

Q4 Some people believe that increased computerisation in the workplace will cause more unemployment. Write a brief explanation of this point of view.

Get lost. I'm on my tea-break.

....

....

....

....

Section Eight — Business and Change

New Technology — E-commerce

Q1 Write down the two main aspects to the internet.

a) ....

b) ....

Q2 How can credit card numbers be made secure when buying a product online? Explain how the software works.

....

....

....

Q3 Complete the following sentences, using words from the box to fill in the spaces.

> internet user   telephone operators
> fixed costs   company   post

Businesses can reduce some of their .... by conducting

their business over the internet. The information is put online so that the

.... pays the cost rather than the

.... This means that firms do not need to send

information by .... Companies can also dispense with

.... by putting information online.

Q4 Tick whether the following statement is true or false.
If it is false write the correct version and explain your answer.

> The increase in e-commerce means that brand image is becoming less and less important.

True ☐   False ☐

....

....

....

Section Eight — Business and Change

Globalisation

Q1 What is integration? Write a brief explanation in the space below.

....

....

....

Q2 Tick whether the following statement is true or false.
If it is false write the correct version and explain your answer.

> Companies are increasingly using different brand names for one product to tailor a campaign to a particular country.

True ☐   False ☐

....

....

....

Q3 Fill in this table by writing in good points and bad points about globalisation.

Good points	Bad points

My mum went to the Arctic Circle and all I got was this can of Coke...
You can buy some products almost everywhere in the world. Personally I find it all a little bit scary — I know people who travel abroad and only ever eat in McDonalds restaurants. Nice.

Section Eight — Business and Change